EASY READING INFORMATION SERIES

SOAP

Written by O. B. Gregory
Illustrated by Denis Wrigley

Library of Congress Cataloging in Publication Data

Gregory, O. B. (Olive Barnes), 1940-
  Soap.

  (Easy reading information series)
  Summary: Describes how soap is made by hand
and by machine from oil pressed from nuts and seeds
and mixed with other materials. Includes questions
and vocabulary.
  1. Soap—Juvenile literature.   [1. Soap]
I. Wrigley, Denis, ill.   II. Title.   III. Series.
TP991.G66   668'.124   81-11892
ISBN 0-86625-168-5   AACR2

ROURKE PUBLICATIONS, INC.
Windermere, Fla. 32786

SOAP

Soap is very important to us.

It helps us to be clean.

We wash ourselves with it.

We wash clothes with it.

It also helps us
    to keep our homes clean.

This is the story
    of how soap is made.

Soap is made from oils and fats.

The oils and fats
come from animals or vegetables.

The vegetable oils
come from trees or plants.

The trees or plants have seeds.

The oil is inside the seeds.

The picture shows a palm tree.

Oil from the nuts of palm trees
is used for making soap.

Another kind of vegetable oil
        comes from ground-nuts.

The oil comes from the seeds.

The seeds are in the pods.

The pods come after the flowers
        which grow near the ground.

The flower bends over
        and pushes into the ground.

The pods grow in the ground.

Another name for ground-nuts
        is monkey nuts.

The seeds come from
all over the world.

Palm oil comes from West Africa
and Malaysia.

Ground-nuts come from West Africa.

Coconuts come from
islands in the Pacific Ocean.

Palm trees and ground-nuts
need a warm or hot country.

To get the oil out the seeds
  must be pressed. The oil is
  squeezed out and shipped to
  other countries.

Sometimes it is sent as a liquid.

Sometimes it is sent as a solid fat.

Sometimes the seeds are sent.

The picture shows a large ship
  delivering nuts.

They will be sent to a mill
  to have the oil pressed out.

The oil is now taken
to the soap factory.

It is put in a big tank.

The tank is called a soap pan.

A kind of alkali
is now mixed with the oil.

The oil and alkali
are heated a little.

The picture shows a soap pan.

The man at the side can tell
when the oil and alkali
are mixed.

The oil and alkali mix together
and become soap and glycerine.

Then salt water is added.

The glycerine sinks to the bottom.

The soap rises to the top
and is drawn off.

Sometimes it is put into tanks
where it cools and sets hard.

The soap is then cut into bars
by strong wires.

This is the old way
of making bars of soap.

The new way of making soap
    is to do almost everything
    by machine.

Hot fat, oil and water
    are pumped into a hydrolyzer.

A hydrolyzer is a tall steel tube
    about as wide as a barrel.

Water goes in at the top.

Oil and fat go in at the bottom.

After a time, a fatty acid
    rises to the top.

Glycerine and water sink
    to the bottom.

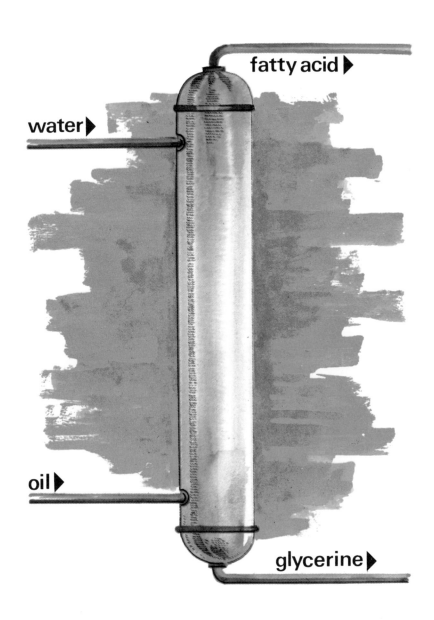

The fatty acid is then purified.

Other things are added to it
   to make it into soap.

Sometimes perfume and color
   are put in.

The soap is made in one long bar.

It has to be cut into single bars.

It is cut into single bars by machine.

Look at the picture.

You can see bars of soap.
   They have been cut and packaged.

The soap is now sent to stores.

People buy it.

Bars of soap are used
for hand washing and bathing.

Different types of soap are
used for laundry. Shampoo
is used to wash hair.

THINGS TO WRITE

1. What is soap made from? (4)

2. What do vegetable oils come from? (4)

3. Where is the oil? (4)

4. Where do the ground-nut pods grow? (6)

5. What is another name for ground-nuts? (6)

6. Where does palm oil come from? (8)

7. Where do ground-nuts come from? (8)

8. Where do coconuts come from? (8)

9. What sort of country do palm trees need? (8)

10. Where are the ground-nuts sent? (10)

11. Where is the oil taken? (12)

12. What is the big tank called? (12)

13. What is mixed with the oil? (12)

14. What do the oil and alkali become? (14)

15. What else is put in? (14)

16. What happens to the soap? (14)

17. What is the new way of making soap? (16)

18. What is a hydrolyzer? (16)

19. How is the soap cut into single bars? (18)

20. What is shampoo used for? (20)

VOCABULARY

PALM — a tall tree with leaves at the top, usually grown in tropical climates.

GLYCERINE — a sweet, colorless substance which is easily dissolved in water.

POD — a container, usually oval in shape, which holds seeds.

ALKALI — a substance which neutralizes acids to form salts.

PERFUME — a substance usually made from the extract of flowers or fruits. It has a pleasant smell. It makes soap smell good.

PURIFY — to make clean. Example: a water purifier takes all the dirt and mineral deposits out of water and leaves it clean.